Not So Different After All

Welcome to the World of Sheep

Not So Different After All

Welcome to the World of Sheep

Kate Ripley

ISBN: 9798846104396

Table of Contents

Introduction

The Animal Welfare (Sentencing) Bill which recognises animals as sentient beings received Royal Assent in April 2021. It is a further stepping stone in the development of our understanding of the evolutionary continuity that exists between humans and other animals. Historically, there have been attempts to draw a clear red line between humans and the rest of the animal kingdom but the evidence from neurology, physiology and the study of animal behaviour has gradually eroded that boundary.

One of the last bastions of the dichotomy was the idea of 'man the toolmaker'. In 1960, Jane Goodall observed chimpanzees in Gombe using a stick as a tool to reach termites in their mound. This discovery prompted her mentor, Louis Leakey, to assert that ' now we must redefine tool, redefine man or accept chimpanzees as human.'

Much of the work exploring animal intelligence and self awareness has been done with our close relatives, the primates, but other species have also been shown to share many human attributes including my perhaps unlikely candidates, sheep.

Fortunately, our understanding has moved a long way from the early assertions by philosophers that animals lack conscious awareness. Descartes (17 c) even asserted that the terrified screams of a cat that he threw from a window were only 'mechanical reactions'. A further line of thinking sought to draw a clear distinction between humans and the rest of the animal world by arguing that conscious thought involving concepts was only possible through the medium of language.

As a psychologist with a specialism in developmental language disorders and autism, I have carried out hundreds of psychometric assessments of children and young people who have little or no understanding of language (receptive disorder) and/ or ability to use language in order to communicate (expressive disorder). Standard psychometric assessments such as the British Ability Scales have separate verbal and non-verbal (Performance)scales. One of my tasks ,early in my career, when working in an assessment centre was to identify individuals who had average non-verbal ability and were, therefore, considered to be able to benefit from education in a specialist school for those with developmental language disorders. The evidence accumulated over time showed that children with little or no language ability were able to obtain average scores for their age on the non-verbal scales. However, beyond the primary school years their age related scores began to fall below their own previous scores and those of their more language skilled peers (Ripley, 2008). Many of the non-verbal tasks are timed and quick responses earn bonus points. The evidence suggests that language does mediate efficient problem solving as non-verbal tasks become more complex and demanding. However, it is possible to achieve success with tasks from the Performance Scales such as block design or matrices without the concepts being framed by language.

Developments in neuropsychology have made it increasing untenable to attempt to distance humans from other animals. The Cambridge Declaration (2012) stated that non human animals have the same neuroanatomical, neurochemical and neurophysiological substrates of conscious states and the capacity to exhibit intentional behaviour. There are homologous brain circuits in humans and animals that correlate with conscious experience and perception. While neural circuits in the sub- cortical regions support attention, sleep and decision making. The evidence that the emotional feelings of humans and non humans arose from homologous sub cortical brain networks is further support for the idea of parallel evolutionary development.

De Waal (2003) recognises that the complex cognitive capacities that we boast as human have evolved over time and that there is likely to be a continuum of development between humans and other animals. All animals need a self concept, to know about themselves, in order to thrive in their physical and social environment. He considers all animals to be conscious thinking beings able to prioritise information for appropriate action. There is still no clear understanding of how consciousness in humans arises from the neural activity of the brain but ,unlike animals, humans can use language to describe their conscious experiences.

The Cambridge Declaration (2012) asserted that humans are not unique in possessing the neurological substrates that generate consciousness. De Grazia (2009) writes that the evidence makes it more reasonable to accept that animals are self aware than to deny that thesis. This book takes as it's theme the three types of self awareness that are described by de Grazia; body self awareness, social self awareness and introspective awareness. Each type is considered with reference to sheep a species that is often dismissed as stupid. There is, perhaps, a surprisingly extensive catalogue of research evidence about the behaviour of sheep. In the book the research evidence is presented supported by case studies of the behaviour of my flock of Shetland sheep.

My first three sheep came from a friend in 1988. She recommended the Shetland breed as small for handling, hardy and choosing to eat most weeds in preference to grass. She was right. The sheep cleared dock leaves in Sussex and Hampshire but for some reason ignore them in Devon. Perhaps the soil type changes the flavour and makes them less palatable.

In 1988 Shetlands were on the rare breeds list, another reason for my choice. Since then they have become popular particularly among smallholders and have their own breed society. My original cast of characters is now long gone but the present generation features in the form of both case studies and photographs.

To be registered with a breed society sheep have to have names. Most flocks use a different letter each year for their cohort of lambs. Some letters are easier than others to mine for names. We once bought two ewes from a flock for which the letter for that year was Q. Queenie was obvious, Quean less so and a large cohort must have presented a challenge. After a move to Hampshire, we decided to expand the flock and I chose to name my sheep according to their maternal blood line. This makes it easier to identify individuals in terms of their family group when studying social behaviour. The names of the sheep that appear in the text reflect their dynasty. My first dynasty was ' rocks and minerals' with Ruby as the matriarch. Olivia was the matriarch of the 'Shakespeare' line and one of her descendants, Oberon, is a prominent character in my cast. Omo is the matriarch of the 'cleaning products' line who we acquired in the same year, from the same breeder, as Olivia. Queenie started the 'regal' line and Grebe is the oldest survivor of the 'birds'. Other blood lines like the 'trees and shrubs' have died out with their last survivor , Juniper, who never gave us a ewe lamb to continue her dynasty.

Shetlands have a clear advantage when carrying out behavioural observations because they are easy to identify by the colour of their fleeces and individual markings. They range from white (Omo) through shades of brown and grey to black (Perdita). It is, therefore, easy to record who is grazing or resting together using the Proximity Index. For this measure, I focus on a target sheep and record the two that are closest to them whether grazing or resting. Analysis of the data for each individual reveals consistent affiliations between the flock members The importance of family ties within the flock is made clear from this observational data. There is more going on in a flock than most people realise as sheep make choices about what to eat, where to go and who to hang out with. Self awareness is the focus of the book.

Part One

Body Self-awareness

All animals that move around in their environment have an awareness of their own body in space through proprioception. Proprioceptors are present in muscles and joints to provide information which helps to develop a body image of where different parts of the body are relative to the environment. A clear image of body boundaries contributes to the development of spatial awareness in the surroundings. For sheep this might be finding a small gap in a hedge through which to explore a different field. When proprioception is efficient constant small adjustments are made to maintain balance and posture while moving over uneven ground. For most people and animals these adjustments are made without conscious awareness but for people with disorders such as Developmental Coordination Disorder the fine adjustments command conscious attention (Ripley, 2015). Lambs quickly develop motor skills that it takes human infants years to acquire.

The ability to interpret the signals that come from one's own body is known as Interoception (Schauder et al. 2015). Animals show awareness of the signals of pain or discomfort in their bodies through their behaviour -bottle fed lambs vocalise loudly when they are hungry. The first signs of illness or infection are shown by changes in behaviour. A limp is the obvious sign of a foot infection or the need for a trim while subtle changes in posture can indicate a case of fly strike that needs immediate treatment.

In humans interoceptive ability varies so that some individuals on the autism spectrum have a reduced ability which can lead to signs of illness or injury going unreported, sometimes with serious consequences that can include a reduced life span.(Ripley, 2019). Children may need prompting to put on a coat when it is snowing outside or to shed layers when it is hot. Sheep are quick to seek shade on a hot day and run for cover when it rains if a shelter is available.

Too wet out there

Olfactory Awareness: Smell

The external receptors for vision, smell, taste and hearing are shared by humans and sheep but they ascribe different levels of significance to the information from these sources. In humans vision is the dominant sense with which to interpret incoming information but in many animals smell may trump vision or be needed to confirm visual information. Both dogs and sheep fail the mirror test (more

4

of which later) but they do identify themselves and others by smell.

When foraging, sheep select plants to eat initially by smell but prefer sweet and sour tastes to bitter. Ginane (2011) found evidence that sheep categorise plant species according to their botanical family and they will self medicate by seeking out plants to meet their needs (Villalba 2006).

Oberon is a ram who never really grew despite having a hearty appetite. A metabolic disorder is suspected but there is no clear diagnosis. During lockdown because of the corona virus epidemic I started to take him for walks, as a dog substitute.

Out walking on his lead rope, Oberon seeks out yellow and white flowers and has developed a liking for hogweed which has superseded his previous preference for sycamore. Species rich lawn grass is preferable to anything found in a sheep field.

Oberon out for a browse

Kendrick (1997) describes how important smell is in forming an initial bond between ewes and their lambs. Shepherds have long exploited this when they foster lambs onto a ewe.

Ariel was a bottle fed rejected twin and I was anxious about how she might take to a mothering role because of this. When I went to check her, I could see a nose still in the membrane and decided that she needed help. I managed to free the lamb's nose but Ariel kept on turning to me to lick my hands so it was not possible to assist the lamb. The fact that she was licking in response to the smell on my hands was an encouraging sign that the instinct to lick off a lamb was active. I set off up the field to get help to hold her. She ran up the field after me and to the surprise of us both, out popped the lamb. I stayed with her while she licked him off and had his first, colostrum, feed as she clearly wanted her foster mother as her birth partner.

Ariel with Buster

Sheep have scent glands in front of their eyes and between their digits which give each animal an individual signature smell. Social greetings between sheep often involve sniffing the faces of flock mates to reinforce the existing bonds. Humans are seldom aware of using smell to identify others unless they are aware of a signature perfume or are in an intimate relationship

Vomeronasal organs of rams detect the pheromones of ewes in oestrus and they show the same sniffing pose as that seen in horses or dogs. However, it often seems that the ewes take the initiative by standing provocatively close to the fence line.

Auditory Awareness: Hearing

Sheep are alert to their auditory environment and will show hyper vigilance in response to the unfamiliar sounds of new surroundings.

In Hampshire the home field was close to RAF Odiham and the sheep learned to ignore the sounds of Chinook helicopters. As humans, we were aware that increased activity usually heralded some action abroad that would be reported in the news about a week later but the sheep were not bothered. However, each year some of the vintage aeroplanes that took part in the Farnborough air show were based at Odiham and the sheep were spooked by the different sounds from the sky.

In a familiar field with good sight lines vocalisations may be infrequent but the incidence increases when they are moved to new pasture or the sight lines are restricted. One hot summer when the grazing was limited we let the sheep into the copse and the number and amplitude of contact calls increased dramatically.

Contact calls are distinct from alarm calls and those that alert other flock members to assemble at the feeding pen. Each sheep has it's individual voice that is recognised by both humans and flock members (Kendrick1995).

Although smell is important for post parturition bonding, after a short time, vocal and visual recognition become more significant . There is a peak of vocal activity between ewes and lambs in the first three hours after birth and just prior to nursing (Sebe et al. 2008). The ewe vocalises ten times more frequently than the lamb in the early stages which helps the lamb to recognise its mother's voice. The ewe makes low pitch vocalisations, mouth closed for near contact signalling. These low frequency sounds are heard in utero and may have a reassuring, calming effect on the new born.

Also, these sounds do not 'travel' and thereby alert predators to the location of the lamb. Experienced ewes make fewer high pitched bleats than first time mothers. Singleton and first born lambs have a lower bleat rate than second born twins that are already competing for maternal attention. Neglected or separated lambs bleat loudly and bottle fed lambs have particularly penetrating calls at feeding time.

As prey animals, ewes usually retire to a secluded spot and the birth process is conducted quietly with low pitched bleats. Frequent checking that the process is going according to plan is necessary because of the reluctance to draw attention to vulnerability. However, some ewes do not adhere to this sensible practice.

Perdita a confident bottle fed ewe decided to have her lamb in the field shelter in the yard. Loud noises like labour enacted in an episode of 'Casualty' alerted me to investigate. She had a quick easy birth by most standards and her bouncing Ben (Benedict) is the only lamb I have seen jump on his mother's back while she was standing up.

Perdita

Visual Awareness

Humans, primates and other predators like cats have eyes that face forward and are able to achieve binocular vision (Ripley, 2005) which facilitates accommodation for near vision. Sheep have eyes on the side of their heads and are able to see behind without moving their heads. This is a useful adaptation for prey animals and sheep don't need to read much. In 1970's it was interesting to learn how horses and sheep had a 'ramp retina' to achieve accommodation to objects at various distances and I assumed that this was some sort of anatomical difference in the structure of the eye. However, Fails & McGee (2018) explain that the so called 'ramp retina' is the result of photoreceptors that synapse with other neurons within the retina so that visual information undergoes early neural processing within the retina. A change of focus, accommodation, is achieved by eye and head movement.

As humans we are used to having a full range of colour receptors, unless suffering from the genetic condition of 'colour blindness'. For sheep , blue and yellow are perceived best against their backdrop of green vegetation and brown soil. Yellow and blue buckets were, therefore, my chosen props for early problem solving experiments and we know to wear dark sludge green and brown when working in the bush.

The evidence suggests that sheep and humans share similar information from their senses. However the weighting that they give to the different senses in order to interpret their environment is different. Beckoff (2005) advises human investigators to drop their visual bias and understand that for animals such as dogs and sheep smell may have greater salience. He suggests that animals integrate information from all their senses in order to operate successfully in their environment.

For de Grazia body self-awareness, the first of his three types of self awareness, gives agency to individuals as they move around and act on their environment.

Social Self Awareness

Social self awareness is the second of the three types of self awareness identified by de Grazia and sheep are highly sociable flock animals. The early bonding between ewes and their lambs continues throughout life if they are able to remain together. Rowell (1991) describes this bond in a paper entitled 'Till death do us part'.

Up the sheep track in single file came Jet followed by her daughter Chrystal, followed by her daughter Onyx while the youngest, Sapphire brought up the rear. Resting by the feed pen one morning, lying together were the pairings of Robin with 3 month old Owl, Linnet with her year old Dove and Breeze with her yearling F-G (Fairy Glen). The other youngest lambs were with their mothers in the field shelter.

Family groups do habitually graze together as shown by the Proximity Index (Ripley 2020). They may disperse in familiar surroundings but come back together when they are anxious. Sheep society within the flock is based on affiliative bonds which may include friends from their lamb cohort as well as relatives. Boissy & Durant (2002) found that sheep graze longer and are less vigilant when they are with familiar companions and split more easily into sub groups for handling. It follows that if sheep have to move to a new home they will settle more quickly and thrive if they have the support of their family group.

For most people a sheep is a sheep but like other mammals they show personality traits that are consistent over time (Marino, 2019). Boldness in sheep was judged by Sibbald (2009) as willingness to leave the group. Omo, one of our older ewes is friendly towards humans but can be independent and adventurous. It took us a while to realise that she was leading her daughter and two lambs out under the gate to browse on the farm track. She led them back in time for tea except the day when we were early and caught her leading them back.

Some sheep are more gregarious and spend more time in close proximity to others and they are often in the front of the group when there is an 'agreed' movement of the whole flock (Ramseyer 2009). Others are more anxious about changes of routine and the presence of strangers.

Jet is a complex character who is friendly and confident when there is a well established routine. A change of field may precipitate a crisis of confidence and a refusal to follow the rest of the flock. She spent a day on her own until the lure of a pot of nuts and the sight of all the others in the feeding pen persuaded her to go out of one gate, into the yard and through the adjacent gate. One year the sheep had been penned for shearing but rain cancelled the arrangement and they were let out. Jet refused to be penned again and despite all our efforts did not get sheared that year. She will do anything to avoid being caught if she is limping and her feet need attention.

Jet

There are dominance hierarchies within the ewe flock but this is less significant than within a group of rams (Shackleton & Shank 1984). Rams can be quite brutal with weaker flock mates especially when deposing a previously dominant individual. The hierarchy within the ewe flock can change over time and there were frequent butting incidents when Grebe was deposed as the dominant ewe.

It is clear from observing their behaviour and noting the different personalities that sheep recognise each other as individuals. Marino (2019) reported that sheep can recognise up to fifty individuals for over two years even if they have been separated during that time.

Individual personalities are much in evidence at lambing time. Some ewes are protective and keep their lambs under close supervision. Amber climbed on the muck heap to monitor her twins, Jasper and Zircon, when they went off to play with Lisa and Robin who were older. Ophelia was less concerned when Puck and Celia joined the others but chased away the cat when he came too close. Crystal went off down the field leaving Quartz and Tiffany with the lamb group but she did go in search of Tiffany, calling loudly, when she had strayed into the next field. In contrast, it was several days before Onyx allowed Sapphire to stray more than a metre away without calling to her or going to fetch her.

Lambs at play on a muck heap

Sometimes history repeats itself and a ewe rejects one of her twins. Breeze had twins for her second pregnancy and rejected Ariel the first born. She reared Ajax and left the mothering of Ariel to us. We lamb the ewes every other year and she had twins again. This time she accepted Fairy the first born and left us to rear Surf. Most ewes are willing to look after twins and Breeze is healthy, bigger than her

16

mother- Omo. On what did she base her decision? Neither birth order nor gender was consistent in her choice.

The evidence is that sheep recognise each other as individuals and develop long term relationships with their flock mates. It is not surprising, therefore, that they react to death by showing similar behaviour to that reported for elephants. Fortunately, deaths in the field are rare.

Shaun had gradually become blind in his later years but in a familiar field he was able to find his way around and respond to the sound of shaken bucket. When he died in the field the two wethers who had been his companions were standing close by and occasionally nuzzling him.

Two ram lambs, Slate and Puck had gone with their mothers and twin sisters to a new home. One morning a year later we had a call to say that Slate, apparently healthy the night before, was dead in the field. Puck was nuzzling him and pawing him as if, they said, he was trying to wake him up.

Social Communication

Humans and other animals that live in social groups develop strategies with which to regulate their social encounters. For humans language dominates but eye gaze and body language are also essential components of an interaction. They may even 'leak' a message that is at variance with the words that are spoken. The importance of non- verbal communication in the smooth regulation of social interactions is evident in the difficulties experienced by some people on the autism spectrum (Ripley, 2009). Sheep do have individual voices but most of their close encounters are regulated by body language and smell. There are differences between friendly and potentially aggressive encounters signalled by ear and face posture and head angle (Reefman 2009).

For a friendly encounter sheep approach slowly to about one metre apart, halt and then advance slowly, ears forward, nose forward of the vertical. They sniff noses and align their faces side on to engage the scent receptors beneath the eyes.

Mica and Nickel, cousins, spent long sessions side on side rubbing shoulders, neck and heads while making huffing and grunting noises. They would both raise the front leg next to the other and make a pawing gesture. This pawing is most commonly made when a more dominant sheep approaches a subordinate but with non aggressive intent. It may serve to engage the scent glands between the toes.

The prelude to an unfriendly encounter is signalled by the halt one metre apart but with ears back and the nose behind the vertical. They may charge immediately or, commonly in rams, move backwards a few paces to maximise the impact of the charge.The behaviour may continue for some time with head on clashes punctuated by side swipes. An initial one on one battle may be joined by others both in the ram and ewe flock.

Field notes - February 2020

Onyx and Beryl having a stand off. Breeze joined the fray and she with Onyx chased Beryl away. Tiffany and Ophelia head bobbing and pawing. Viola, mother of Ophelia came over and chased Tiffany away.

Face Recognition

Keepers of sheep will be aware that they recognise individual humans (Davis et al.1998) and all but the most anxious animals will approach their carers with ears and nose pointing forward. The boldest regularly paw humans in the hope of being given treats. If strangers are present the sheep show vigilant behaviour and avoid eye contact.

Banjo

Sheep recognise carers that they have not seen for some time. As Kendrick (2001) reports ' sheep do not forget a face'. Banjo came to us for stud duty and stayed on because his owner had health issues. It was over a year before she was able to visit him. As we walked to the field she said with sadness that he would come to me not her because I had been feeding him. We walked into the field side by side and to her delighted amazement Banjo went straight up to her.

A twin study reported in The Psychologist, 2015, had found that most of the genes associated with face recognition are different from those involved in general mental ability. It is argued that face recognition is a special skill that has evolved separately from other mental abilities. It is an ability shared by humans and sheep.

Symbolic Representation:

The evidence that sheep recognise and remember the faces of sheep and humans is irrefutable but the surprising evidence is that sheep understand symbolic representation in the form of photographs of humans and sheep (Knolle 2017).

Presented with a two entry maze puzzle to access a reward, sheep will choose the route marked with the photograph of a familiar sheep or human rather than that of a stranger. The sheep respond to the photographs using visual cues from the faces and have specialised neural systems in the temporal and frontal regions of the brain to perform the task. As with humans, there is some degree of right hemisphere specialisation for face identification (Broad et al. 2000).

A group of sheep that had been used for cognitive testing had learned to respond to letters presented on a computer screen. They were then presented with photographic images of sheep, familiar humans and celebrities who they had never seen in life. They were able to recognise the individuals from the photographs and even recognise the images when they were presented from different perspectives. This skill had only previously been demonstrated in humans and their drop in performance of

15% with the perspective shift was similar to that recorded for humans (Knolle et al. 2017).

The face sensitive neural systems also categorise faces in terms of their emotional and behavioural significance (Kendrick et al. 2001). Faced with the maze choice, sheep follow the path marked by a photograph of an unstressed unfamiliar sheep in preference to that of a stressed flock mate (Elliker 2005). For human images, they will follow the pathway signalled by their carer provided that they look relaxed. Faced with a photograph of the carer looking angry they will choose the path marked by a relaxed stranger (Vandenheede 1994)

The close links between the brain regions that control face recognition and the emotional responses in sheep and humans may become dysfunctional in human developmental disorders such as autism (Ripley 2012) but I have not met an autistic sheep.

Symbolic representation is not confined to understanding photographs. Oberon, the ram who never grew because of undiagnosed metabolic disorder, responds to the sight of his rope by running up the field in anticipation of a walk. He was a dog substitute during the Coronovirus lockdown and enjoyed being taken out to browse.

Oberon visiting the neighbours

All sheep seem to understand the significance of a bucket and I remember being amused by a cartoon in an old copy of Punch which depicted a burglar who had been carrying a bag marked 'swag' flattened by a flock of sheep. The farmer was explaining to a bemused looking policeman that the animals had thought he was carrying a bag of feed.

Sheep are at their most comfortable and relaxed with flock mates in a familiar environment. Sheep experiencing stress because of isolation make frequent loud calls, rapid repetitive movements while their heart rate and the levels of stress hormones, cortisol and adrenalin, all increase

(Parrott et.al. 1998). However, if they are able to see pictures of other sheep, particularly familiar sheep, the stress level indicators reduce (Da Costa 2004). Images of their own breed are the most effective (Boissiou 1996) but images of other breeds are more soothing than those of goats or inverted triangles.

Eye Gaze

As a practicing psychologist, I have long been aware of how eye gaze regulates the social interactions between people. A sustained gaze may indicate attraction, potential aggression or a bid for dominance depending on the context and associated body language. The engagement and disengagement of eye contact is used to regulate conversational exchanges and interactions can feel uncomfortable if one partner finds it hard to follow the unwritten rules. People on the autism spectrum can find gaze regulation during conversation a difficult skill and may feel more comfortable avoiding eye contact., The avoidance of eye contact is popularly associated with telling lies unless the liar is well practiced. However, they may betray themselves by overcompensating and holding the eye contact a little too long. It has been shown that solving problems such as mental arithmetic is facilitated if the subject averts their gaze in order to concentrate. In humans , therefore, eye gaze has an important role to play in social encounters and can even be used for social manipulation. The evidence suggests that sheep too are sensitive to the messages of eye gaze both from other sheep and from humans.

Humans, like other predators, have two forward facing eyes and direct gaze indicates to the observed that they are being watched. Sheep as highly vigilant social prey animals use visual cues to detect potential danger (Dwyer, 2004). Direct eye contact, staring, by humans or other sheep is seen as a signal that some kind of interaction is about to take place. The nature of that potential interaction is, as with humans, signalled by the associated body language. Sustained eye contact between two sheep, ears back, head behind the vertical may be the prelude to a butting contest. A less dominant animal may interpret this as the time to take evasive action.(Kendrick,1991). In contrast, eye contact between two animals approaching slowly with nose and ears forward might signal a friendly encounter with sniffing, grunting and rubbing against each other.

Sheep are aware of the significance of the face when attempting to interpret the intentions of humans. Beausoleil (2005) observed that 80% of glances or stares at humans are directed at the face. The results from the 'Arena Test' demonstrated that eye gaze is an important cue to the possible intentions of an unfamiliar person. For the arena test a stranger stands in a pen with the sheep and either looks directly at them or looks down at the floor. A direct gaze from an unfamiliar person elicited a fear response; retreat and behavioural signs of anxiety. If the stranger stayed calm with an averted gaze the sheep did, after a while, approach and sniff at the person. In contrast, if a familiar carer stood in the arena they would be likely to elicit an immediate approach accompanied by sniffing at pockets and pawing for attention.

In practice, it is soon learned that if you want to catch a sheep it is best to avoid eye contact. They are particularly vigilant if they suspect that they might be a target for treatment.

Matilda was lame out in a field and there was no feeding pen to tip the odds in favour of a successful catch. The strategy that worked was to put down a bucket, she was always keen on her food, and the catcher to stand motionless by the bucket with no eye contact. When she was fully distracted by the food the second person standing watching about three metres away, gave the signal to grab her.

At other times, eye contact by a familiar carer may be perceived as a positive signal by a sheep.

A pot of nuts is often shared by some of the ewes while the feed troughs are being filled.

Ariel waiting to be hand fed sheep nuts

Several of the ewes do respond but bottle fed Ariel is attracted to the pot by direct eye contact which is probably more effective than simultaneously being called by name.

She will also respond to the gaze being directed at a different spot and move to the position indicated. The change of gaze focus is sometimes supplemented by gesture.

The positive response by Quartz to eye gaze is helpful in managing the problem with his horns. At a few weeks old Quartz put his head through the sheep netting and when he pulled back to get out he displaced his horn bed. With the help of the vet his horns were stabilised but they now grow at an angle so they project into his head. Horn trimming has been a regular feature of his life and a trim was needed. At feeding time he was nearest to the pen, so Chris gave him eye contact and opened the hurdle. Quartz obligingly walked in. There are frequent breaks for treats while the sawing takes place as the vibration and noise close to his ear must be unpleasant for him. Unfortunately, the saw blade broke before we could tackle his second horn.

Quartz

26

A week later, with a new stronger hacksaw available, it was time to work on the other horn. Quartz was hanging out with Surf, bottle fed rejected twin of Breeze and Benedict, the bouncing son of Perdita. I went into the feed pen looked straight at him and called his name. Despite his recent previous experience, Quartz walked over to the pen and I gave him a reward before going to fetch Chris with the new hacksaw. He really is remarkably tolerant of his horn trimming experiences and there are many of the others that it would be difficult to hold still for such an operation.

One experienced, confident wether, Shaun, was able to take advantage of his understanding of eye gaze. Shaun would approach people even if there were visitors in the group. It took some time to work out why small children ended up on the ground crying - no one saw Shaun knock them over. He only did it when no adults were watching. His targets were always children whose eye level was at or below his own. Eventually, we realised what was happening and stayed vigilant when small visitors were present.

For both humans and sheep eye gaze is an important signal that is used to regulate social encounters. How individuals, sheep or human, interpret eye gaze as a potential threat or promise will depend on the context of the encounter, the associated body language and who is making the eye contact.

Teachers, sheep and Paddington bear

Know how to use the 'hard stare'

Playful Lambs

In Spring people delight in watching lambs at play. Lambs like other young animals have to learn how to play. Twins are aware of each other almost immediately because they share the space next to their mother. Singletons stay close to their mothers who often keep them away from the lamb mix in the early days so it is possible to observe the development of their play skills.

Field notes: April 2019.

Matilda gave birth to Lisa (Adelisa) and Grebe to Robin the same morning. For the first two days they stayed close to their mothers and by day three they moved around more but there was no lamb with lamb interaction. On days four and five they were roaming more independently and some lamb on lamb following was observed. By day six they were turn taking in parallel play jumping on and off the muck heap. By day seven reciprocal play was established with head bobbing and pawing as they scaled the muck heap. At ten days they joined forces to round up the chickens in a coordinated enterprise.

Friends - Robin with Adlisa

Indoor Play

Time for a rest

They gradually became more independent- going under the fence into the next field and playing on a tree stump. Twins born seventeen days after Lisa and Robin were joining in the muck heap game at six days old, following the same time scale for the development of their play.

The gradual development of play skills moving from parallel play to reciprocal play follows the same pattern as for humans but at an accelerated pace. Marino et al.(2019) identified gender differences in play so that for males butting and mounting were more common while ewe lambs gambolled and frolicked more. Both were seen to buck and whirl. Gender differences have been described in the play of children although many of these are now ascribed to differences in socialisation.

We usually think of mature sheep as staid animals but as twilight falls our ewes are often seen racing and leaping in the field while the rams engage in chasing and jousting.

Intelligent Sheep: An Oxymoron?

Animal intelligence has been defined as the ability to deal with species specific challenges (Safini 2015). Feral sheep have well developed navigation skills and a memory for which part of the territory is their home range. Hill farmers know the value of a hefted flock whose ewes pass on the territorial knowledge to their offspring.

Even young animals can demonstrate an amazing ability to navigate their environment.

The twin bottle fed lambs tracked us down a field on the opposite side of the dividing fence. They ran down through three paddocks at 90 degrees to come up under a gate to join us in the original field. We all then went through the copse and across a stream to inspect the hay cut. They came back with us except for a detour under a fence to avoid a muddy gateway.

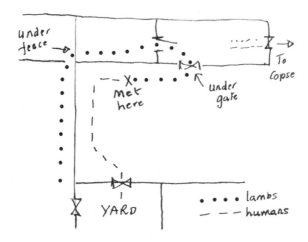

In early times shepherds would have led their flocks in a fence free environment so perhaps one of the greatest challenges for sheep has been to adapt to their role as farmed animals kept in fields.

The ability to recognise sheep and humans over time in vivo and from photographs demonstrates competent memory skills. Sheep demonstrate both recognition and recall memory in a range of environmental contexts.

Sheep are particularly good at remembering routines especially when food is involved. Our flock will assemble at their feeding pens at about 5:00pm, clock time, regardless of the variation in light levels over the year in our latitude. How do they do this? A change of field involves a change of feeding pen and once they have been shown the new routine they follow it without fail.

Prince, the patriarch ram, had his own individual routine. He was fed apart from the others in a hurdle pen on a black dustbin lid. When he went away on stud duty he took his lid with him so that he would be easy to pen to bring home. As he got older we dispensed with the pen and he would go and eat wherever his lid was put down.

Prince

Our neighbour invites the rams into her chicken enclosure to browse on scrub that she wants cleared. I helped her to encourage the three who had been in there the previous year to go through the narrow gate and they were cool about it. Later that week, I introduced Surf and Ben to the enclosure on their own as the others decided to stay in the cool of the field shelter. The next day we led them all to browse and after that they queued up each morning to go into 'chicken land' and at the gate each evening to be let out for tea.

When the ewe flock is in the far field we usually walk through the copse at feeding time unless we are delivering new supplies. To our surprise Omo quickly recognised the car in the lane and would run down to the gate before we even got out. The others soon took a cue from her and would follow her down. It was then easier to put the sacks of feed on the gate and climb over rather than open it and risk a mass escape.

Ariel worked out routines for herself. She would follow behind the others to the feeding pen and then double back to me for treats. While the others were milling round waiting to be let in, she would go into a 'v' of hurdles and put her front feet on the hurdle so she was above the crowd if they followed her there for sheep nuts.

The good memory for flock mates, humans and routines extends to places. Sheep are eager to return to fresh familiar pastures but introducing them to somewhere new may require patience. We acquired a new field that could be accessed from their known territory through a copse and across a stream. Despite the lure of a bucket, it was hard to persuade them that this was a good idea. Ariel and Perdita, the bottle fed lambs, had played in the copse while we were putting down stones to make a pathway through the mud and would still follow us through when they had a chance. This proved useful. They led their reluctant flock mates across and once the routine was established the ewes were eager to make the trip even if it had been six months since they had visited that field.

Juniper was getting old and frail and was reluctant to go through the copse. Ariel came back with me three times to guide her through and across the stream. A few days later, in another move, Jet got left behind and panicked. Ariel came with me to coax her across.

Memory skills can also be observed when sheep return to a favoured foraging site as the browse becomes available. Oberon was allowed in the garden while he was bottle fed and he always headed for the crab apple tree when there was fruit. On the rare occasions when he escapes into the garden he always checks out the crabapple tree first.

A Devon hedge with sycamore growing in it separates the yard from the causeway field. The muck heap is against the hedge on the yard side. Oberon was in the habit of climbing on the muck heap to eat his favourite sycamore leaves but the remaining leaves were now out of reach. He was sitting outside the field shelter while I was mucking out, watched me load the wheelbarrow and go to the muck heap. As soon as I started forking straw onto the heap, he got up, ran to the pile and climbed up to reach the new leaves. He clearly trusted me not to throw dirty bedding on him while he was up there. This behaviour was repeated each time I added to the pile.

I analysed his behaviour in terms of anticipation and problem solving.

- I can reach leaves from the muck heap

- She is making it higher

- I can reach more leaves

- Get up there now

Oberon uses the muck heap to access Sycamore

Worth the climb

If animal intelligence is defined as the ability to deal with species specific problems, Oberon shows good awareness of his environment.

Intelligence Tests for Sheep

Sheep are able to demonstrate problem solving ability within their natural environment and so the next question is to what extent are they able to solve novel problems devised by humans. This approach is borrowed from the realms of human assessment. Binet pioneered the idea of an intelligence test which was a key component of any assessment by an educational psychologist for five decades. The concept of an all embracing 'IQ' began to fall out of favour at the turn of the century as Dynamic Assessment became more popular. However, testing using novel tasks remains central to much research into animal intelligence.

Morton et al. (2011) built their tasks on the premise that the ability to respond to a stimulus, take action and evaluate the outcome to guide future behaviour is a fundamental element for survival in all animals. It is an executive function that breaks down in neurodegenerative diseases such as Huntington's Chorea and Alzheimer's.

They tested the sheep using three paradigms :

1. Simple discrimination between yellow and blue buckets- colours that sheep detect most easily. All fourteen sheep learned that the yellow bucket had the reward and retained that memory for six weeks.

2. Colour reversal condition. The yellow bucket became the incorrect choice. Initially the sheep were confused by the change and showed displacement activity: pawing the trainer, defaecating, urinating and bleating until they learned the reversal after three training sessions.

3. Attentional Shift : A Shape-The stimulus changed from bucket to cone but retained the yellow / blue colour dimension B Colour- The stimulus changed from yellow/ blue bucket to purple/ green bucket

For these demanding shifts of focus, the sheep performed at the same level as humans and macaques. They achieved 80% correct choices by day four as the stimulus dimensions changed by shape(bucket or cone) and by colour (yellow/blue or purple/ green.)

The sheep showed signs of distress and displacement activity at the first set of rule changes but subsequent changes elicited less anxious behaviour. In general the sheep showed a positive response to the testing with ears forward, eye contact and nuzzling the trainer. They seemed to enjoy playing the 'games'!

The rule acquisition behaviour shown by the sheep is an executive function found in humans and monkeys but not in rodents. The sheep acquired the skills more quickly than the monkeys.

The intelligence testing can be done with simple equipment like that used by Morton et al. as not everyone has access to computer screens and infra red sensors as used by Knolle for the discrimination tasks with photographs, shapes and letters. 'Challenge Oberon' kept things simple by using a plank and different shaped plastic boxes.

Task: Identify the box containing the biscuit

- Equipment: three opaque boxes; square, oval, oblong, and a plank to put the boxes on

- Success criterion: push the target box off the plank 100% of trials.

- Method: Show placement of biscuit in box. Place three boxes on the plank

- Rotate the position of the boxes on each trial

Results: Day 1 trials 1-6 random selection, 7-10 100% .By the 4th set of trials 100% correct. The learning was retained with one and two day gaps between trials.

The evidence suggested that his main challenge was not to identify the box that contained the biscuit but to work out that he only got the reward if he knocked the correct box off the plank .The response had to be shaped as I could not explain to him in words what was required!

In humans intelligence is distributed according to the 'normal curve' which means that most people fall within the broadly average range with outliers at the two extremes. Some individuals are exceptionally able while others have ' special needs' in educational terms. The evidence suggests that the same distribution of intelligence applies to sheep. Shaun was exceptionally socially able to take advantage of his ability to understand eye gaze but also often took the lead when the flock was exploring new grazing . Omo recognises the intermittent symbol of a car in the lane as a sign that food supplies are being delivered and runs down to the gate.

In contrast, her great great grandson, Buster, appears to have special needs. He was Ariel's first lamb and has a large head which contributed to the difficult birth. His behaviour suggests that he suffered anoxia, deprivation of oxygen, at birth which has affected his behaviour.

Physically he is well grown but he needs prompts to follow routines and is slow to respond to environmental stimuli and react to the presence of strangers.

Oberon is a year older than Buster and about half the size. The two of them can often be found lying together, nose to tail in the yard or field shelter. They remind me of the duo in the book 'Of Mice and Men'

Oberon with Buster

Self Awareness: The Mirror Test

Sheep show a highly developed level of social and emotional intelligence and understand symbolic representation, so it is hard to comprehend how they have not yet been shown to pass the mirror test. The test was devised by Gallup in 1970 and has for decades been considered as the gold standard for whether animals have an awareness of themselves as individuals. The premise is that once animals have become familiar with a mirror image, a mark is put on their face and if they try to remove it they have passed the test.

Three wethers and five ewes were introduced individually to a mirror mounted on a robust stand. There was considerable variation in response to the image which reflected their personalities. Oberon stared at himself for the longest time, ten minutes. Ariel and Perdita soon lost interest and wandered off to explore the yard while Cloud was fearful of the image. The two lambs, like children under eighteen months, showed no interest in their reflection.

All eight sheep :

1. Initially looked at the image, Cloud from a safe distance.

2. Engaged in ' posing ' behaviour in close contact with the mirror. Posing was defined as making head movements to view the image from different angles.

3. Looked behind the mirror to check if there was another sheep

4. Sniffed the mirror for an extended period, smearing the surface. One hypothesis is that they were trying to engage smell to do a reality test on the visual image.

Lambs took no notice

Beryl looks first

Then she sniffs....

Looks again….

She checks behind before losing interest

One wether showed an immediate aggressive response and one ewe a delayed aggressive response after first posing. In both cases it was not a standard test because there were other familiar sheep reflected in the mirror which might have boosted their confidence.

Oberon showed no interest in a yellow mark on his horn or even when I tied string to it. This raises the question of whether sheep care if they have marks on their faces. They happily ignore brambles and other detritus attached to their wool unless movement is impeded.

The idea that the mirror test is a gold standard for measuring self awareness was questioned when it was found that dogs and cats fail the test but Wrasse, a type of reef fish, pass the test. For dogs and sheep smell may need to supplement vision in order to confirm that the image is 'real' hence the prolonged sniffing behaviour shown by all my sheep. Despite the ability to recognise both sheep and humans from photographs, the integration of information from both senses seems necessary in order to recognise self v not self. De Grazia (2008) concludes that it is 'silly to maintain that passing the mirror test is the only indication of self awareness in animals'

Responses to Threat

Fear is the response to the anticipation of a threat which signals an awareness of the possibility of future pain and implies a sense of self that persists into the future. For de Grazia, this demonstrates that sheep have introspective awareness.

All mammals show three basic responses to threat: fight, flight, freeze. All three may be readily seen in the context of a classroom. A troubled child/ young person will choose to run from the classroom (flight) or down tools, head on the desk and refuse to engage (freeze). Flight is often to a perceived safe place such as under a table or stairs or even up a tree. The message to adults is not to go in after them as this is likely to precipitate a fight response and someone getting hurt.

A fight option is clearly more effective when an animal has claws, teeth, horns or guns that can cause damage. For sheep flight is usually the preferred first option. This reasonable response from a prey animal has , perhaps, contributed to the popular view that they are stupid animals. If flight is not possible, sheep will form a close huddle, weapons (head and horns) pointing outward. This strategy was copied by the waggon trains tracking west across the plains; forming a circle, with weapons, guns, pointing outwards when they came under attack.

Rams and sometimes ewes will choose to fight if a new animal or a returnee is introduced into the flock. Once caught for a procedure such as shearing or foot trimming some sheep go into freeze mode while others will struggle and attempt to fight.

Ewes with lambs may stand at bay, stamp their feet and advance on a perceived threat. This response may be directed at a familiar human, other ewes or smallish potential predators. A ewe can usually defend at least one lamb from a fox in this way.

The occasional sheep will act in an unexpected way :

The home field in Hampshire had a footpath that ran alongside one boundary. We fenced off the pathway to keep dogs and the sheep apart. It was not long before the local dog walkers were talking about a sheep that would approach their dogs at the fence, stamp it's foot and , if the dog did not move away, butt it through the fence. The sheep was Omo who is by no means a large ewe even by Shetland standards.

When we moved to Devon, Omo repeated this pattern of behaviour with the dog next door that was about the same size as her. Perhaps it amused them both. One day Ziggy ,the dog, was standing in the field with her owner chatting to Chris when Omo came up to the group. She initiated the stamp and butt routine and then bit Ziggy. The two were hastily separated before someone got hurt.

Omo

Part Two

My Pathway to Understanding and Valuing Sheep

One of the first pictures of me out of a pram is of feeding a lamb at my aunt's farm. I look like a toddler and the lamb was probably more steady on her feet than me. There is nothing remarkable about what I am doing only about what I am wearing. No child of today would be out in the fields wearing a smocked dress and frilly sun bonnet.

Feeding my first Lamb.

Sadly, I have no memory of feeding the lamb but I have a strong memory of the escaping ram. I always hated being banished upstairs at bedtime and must have tried my mother's patience with my protests and delaying tactics. In bed I could hear the murmur of adult voices downstairs. I didn't feel tired, so why did I have to be excluded?

Even the thick curtains over the window could not disguise the fact that it was still light outside. Gradually, I became aware of a different sound coming from the farmyard outside the window. Curious as ever, I climbed out of bed, scrambled onto the window seat and peered through the curtains.

The noise was coming from a pen in the line of farm buildings across the yard which had poles rather than the walls and doors of the other buildings. I could see directly into the pen at a large, clearly disgruntled ram. He would move back a few paces, lower his horns and charge the poles. For a while, I watched fascinated by his power and determination as the poles shuddered with every charge. (Later in history lessons I had no problem with the concept of a 'battering ram 'as a medieval weapon of war). Off the window seat as the poles began to splinter, run to the top of the stairs and shout 'Mummy'. She came up, settled me back in bed and assured me that the ram could not escape. As soon as she had gone, I was back up to the window. The single minded ram kept up his rhythmic pounding and I could not understand why I was the only one who could hear him. Twice more I called my mother and each time she came upstairs she was, as parents are, increasing irritated. My moment of triumph came when the ram finally broke the poles and headed off out of the yard and off up the lane. This time I was able to shout from the top of the stairs 'The ram is out'.

It was many years later when I had children of my own that I was reminded of the power of a ram. My son and a friend had arranged to take one of my rams to a new home so I shut him in one of the loose boxes for easy loading the next day. He was in the middle of a line of three wooden stables on a brick base. That night I woke several times to the sound of a rhythmic thudding like the sound of a pile driver. I remember thinking it was an odd time to be working on construction, but went back to sleep. The next morning he was still in the stable, the door had held ,but the line of three had been pushed off their brick foundation.

For many years sheep did not feature in my life until, as a teenager, I spent Easter on a farm with a friend and was tutored in tail docking and ringing. This was long before the idea of ear tags. Even then, the memory of sitting on a doorstep consuming a whole Easter Egg at one sitting is the clearer one.

I was an avid watcher of 'One man and his dog 'on the television but because of an interest in dogs rather than sheep. The sheep only came into focus when we went to a local trial in Stanmer Park , near Brighton. The dogs and handlers were less skilled and the ability of a lead sheep to out think the dogs and handlers to organise a breakout was the main entertainment. One parcel of sheep even succeeded in escaping into a wood that backed on to the South Downs. The trial that I watched from the ramparts of Beaumaris Castle when I was a postgraduate student at Bangor was a more professional affair. The setting was amazing with views of the Menai Straights and Snowden on , for once, a clear day.

My next encounter with sheep came when we moved to Chailey along with assorted dogs, cats and ponies. Horses are messy grazers and a friend from the Pony Club suggested that we got some sheep to help with pasture management.It was a close call between Southdown, native to the area, and Shetlands. Both were on the rare breeds list at the time. In the end I chose Shetlands because they were small to handle, had better feet and were less prone to fly strike. I bought two ewes, Brandy and Falla and was given a third more mature ewe, Haggis. Brandy gave me my first lamb who I called Larry after a character in a radio programme Toy Town that featured 'Larry the Lamb'. He had an amazing silver fleece that I had spun to make a jumper.

Peaceful Sheep at Chailey.

For the first two years after I got my sheep compulsory dipping was an annual event. We took the flock over to a friend in the trailer and unloaded them into a covered yard with a concrete floor. Unfortunately, as I executed a sharp turn to cut off an escapee, I slipped, fell and cut my lip on a metal hurdle. I went to the A and E department at Lewes hospital where the local GP on duty sewed up my hare lip.

He had missed a vocation as a surgeon because the repair was almost perfect once the lip had healed. In the meantime, I was forbidden to attempt to talk for. at least ten days. I went to the dentist to have my teeth checked out and handed the receptionist a note explaining what had happened. To my surprise, she started to speak to me loudly and slowly! Even more surprisingly, when I went into the office and greeted a friend and colleague she too began to speak loudly and slowly. She, at least, as the specialist psychologist for the deaf should have known better. I was told that trying to smile with my eyes without the mouth just made me look scared or surprised. Fortunately, I was able to communicate with some Speech and language therapy colleagues by signing rather than having to pass notes which I did at meetings.

The year after my accident, dipping was no longer compulsory and we now all use the spot on prophylactic, Crovect, or Clic to treat animals that get fly strike. This has to be a healthier option for both sheep and people. I remember holidays watching dipping as a child with handlers and by standers being splashed with no thought of protective clothing. Another change over the years has been from routine foot trimming to only attending to the feet of individual animals when they show signs of lameness. The issues around shearing have not changed. It costs more to have sheep sheared than the price of the fleece. Early on , I tried advertising wool in the local paper but paid more for the advertising than I ever got for the fleeces. Some years we even burned fleeces because not even the Wool Board wanted coloured wool. There must some day be a future for wool insulation as an environmentally sustainable option for buildings.

We continued to keep a small flock at Chailey, buying in or borrowing rams as required. I remember my daughters then boyfriend playing matador's with a ram the children had named Danger Mouse after a television cartoon character. It was probably that ram that was co opted into trying the old country cure for dogs that chased sheep. We built a hurdle and bale pen and put the dog and ram in together. They were carefully supervised and no animals were hurt in the process but I can't remember whether the 'cure 'had the desired long term effect. Recently ,I was asked by a neighbour to help her to familiarise her retriever puppy with sheep. Sidney, puppy, was introduced to Oberon (Bron) who I take for walks on a lead rope. The two touched noses and sniffed each other for a while and Sidney licked Bron's nose. All went well until Sidney went into the puppy invitation to play bounce. Bron miss read this as aggression and knocked the puppy over. Sidney lay on his side looking surprised but unhurt. After that the two studiously ignored each other.

My early days with sheep were well supported by friends who were experienced shepherds and I could call upon them for help. However, there came a time when it seemed sensible to enroll with the smallholders course at Plumpton Agricultural College along with a friend who was planning to move to Devon. We thoroughly enjoyed our Wednesday evenings at College and when she moved to Devon we took a trailer load of my Shetlands down to Voley farm to start her flock. The course led to the setting up of the Small Farms Training Group and I remember having an afternoon practicing reversing tractors and trailers. We had a stall at the County Show at Ardingly and I stayed on the committee until we moved.

The next move was to Slyes Farm along with assorted, horses, sheep, dogs, cats and chickens. One early newcomer was an orphan lamb we called Curly. It is interesting how if you have sheep people assume you will be happy to adopt other people's lambs but perhaps they saw me as a soft touch. Curly was very friendly with humans and ran loose in the yard and stables with the dogs. Eventually, my daughter decided that he made a mess in the indoor yard and would have to be banished to join the other sheep in the field. Curly really did not appreciate his change of lifestyle and for many months would run up and down the fence bleating loudly and pathetically whenever he saw a friendly human. It took a long time for him to become part of the flock and ever since we have kept any bottle fed lambs with the flock so that they keep a sheep identity.

Curly with Shaun

Shaun, named by my children after the popular film character, was a friendly wether except where children below his eye level were involved. (His story is told in Part One: Eye Gaze) . For many years he would be the pathfinder who led the flock to explore new quarters when they moved between fields. Later in life, he became blind but he was able to find a bucket of nuts by smell and sound and navigate around a familiar paddock.

More Serious about Sheep

When I moved from Sussex to Hampshire for work we rented a field next to the house to accommodate the sheep and chickens. Chris decided that we should not just have an ageing flock of pets but have lambs again. At the Newbury Show we met Andy Harwood, president of the Shetland Sheep Society and arranged to buy a ram and several ewes from him. This was the start of my dynasties. Most people name the sheep with a letter for the crop of lambs for that year. I decided to give mine family names from the matriarchal line so that for my research purposes it would be easy to identify who was related to whom.

The 'stones and gems 'matriarch was Ruby who lived long enough to baby sit the bottle fed Oberon. Her first daughter was Jet.

Ruby with Jet

I was surprised when Jet's great granddaughter Sapphire was the image of her as a baby. Jet is a complex character who will take nuts from hand but is hyper vigilant if anything out of routine is happening.one year we had the flock penned for the arrival of the shearer but he cancelled at the last minute because of rain. The next day all the sheep came back into the pens for nuts except for Jet who evaded all attempts to lure or drive her in. She carried that fleece all year. The summer of 2022 has been exceptionally hot and so we decided to open up the copse to the ewes . It is cool and shady in there and they love to browse on the trees and shrubs. Twenty eight ewes followed us down the field and followed us down into the copse through the little gate. We shut them out at night and the next morning there was a stampede to be first into the copse. Jet stayed resolutely in the field on her own and did not follow the flock into the copse. She is fourteen now and the path into the copse is steep but she did not go near the gate to check this out. On the fifth day she lingered near the gate until the others had gone down. They were out of sight but she gave some contact calls and headed off up the hill through the trees.

One of Jet's granddaughters, Tiffany was the smallest and liveliest lamb we had. Her twin, Quartz (Eye gaze, part one)caught his small growing horn in the sheep netting and when the vet came to attend to him spotted tiny Tiffany and asked if she was all right. She is now average size and eager for human attention.

The matriarch of the 'Trees and Shrubs 'was Juniper. She never produced any female offspring to continue the dynasty but was eager to try to appropriate someone else's lamb if she did not have one of her own. Juniper was one of only three others who have had problems with lambing. Native breeds are usually independent about having lambs out in the field. I noticed one day that she was getting close to parturition and put her in a small enclosure. We had arranged to meet friends for lunch and nothing seemed urgent. While we were out a neighbour called to say she was in difficulty and I called Ron my 'go to 'shepherd who could get to her before we got back. By the time we had arrived he had helped her deliver healthy twin boys. Dilation of the cervix was the cause of her problem but she went on to deliver two singletons successfully after we moved to Devon. Problems with the dilation of the cervix occurred again at the next pregnancy and we loaded her into the trailer to take her to the vet for medication to dilate the cervix. The vet saved one lamb, male, but her only ever female lamb was the one that did not survive.

The 'Shakespeare 'matriarch was Olivia(Twelfth Night) and her daughter Viola (Twelfth Night) had several successful pregnancies before having to have help to induce parturition and lactation. She accepted Portia(Merchant of Venice) but rejected Perdita (the orphan from Winters Tale). Perdita is a lively assertive character who with Ariel will follow us round the farm and 'help 'with any jobs that we are doing. Trixie(Beatrice ,Measure for Measure) gave us Oberon (Midsummer Nights Dream),from an unplanned pregnancy. Banjo the ram was in a temporary hurdle pen and as we walked down to the yard with some friends who were coming to buy sheep, we saw him jump out of the pen into the ewe field. He got to Trixie before I got to him and the result was August born Oberon. He took some milk from his mother but he gave up following so we took over with the Lamlac. It soon became apparent that he was uncomfortable after feeds and occasionally even lay down and kicked at his stomach. Metacam did seem to ease the symptoms but he did not put on weight like his peers. Eventually, our vet administered a cure for colic in horses which had not been licensed for use with sheep. It worked, no more spasms and he began to put on weight so that he no longer looked like a bag of bones after the latest shearing. We bottle fed Oberon for eight months and usually lambs give up naturally between three to four months. The exception was Jet who let Crystal suckle for almost a year.

The matriarch of the'Royal 'line was Queenie. One of her daughters provided us with the Matilda Mystery which I wrote up for the Shetland sheep society magazine, August 2019. Grebe (Birds , matriarch Quail) and Matilda who by the stage of udder development were close to lambing went off to a quiet corner of the field .Some sheep will go 'on retreat 'up to two days before anything happens so I was not concerned. When we checked later in the day, the two ewes were sitting some distance apart each with a lamb. The lambs were licked off and judging from the condition of the navels, the one with Matilda seemed the younger of the two. The ewes were given water and feed in the field and the lambs were suckling well. There was little interaction with the rest of the flock until day two when they brought the lambs up to the yard to feed with the others. I was interested in when singleton lambs developed interactive play and was keeping detailed field notes about their behaviour. It was twelve days before the rest of the flock started to lamb which was ideal for my study. The surprise came on 30th April, 23 days after the birth of Matilda's first lamb, when I found her licking off twin lambs with all the signs of a recent birth…. the mystery! Two possible scenarios:

1. A case of miss-mothering

The smart money at the local vets was on this option. Hypothesis- Grebe has twins and Matilda appropriates one of them and starts to lactate. Problems:

A. If one twin is taken it is usually the first born while the ewe licks off the second. Inspection of the navels had suggested that the one with Matilda was the younger of the two.

B. Ewes will start to lactate for an adopted lamb but usually when they are close to giving birth themselves. Matilda gave birth to twins 23 days later.

Prof Mills, Specialist in Behavioural Veterinary Medicine, University of Lincoln found it strange that she produced milk so early unless it was a case of super fecundity.

2. Super fecundity.

Prof Mills again : I have heard of some animals conceiving on a different cycle and so giving birth twice. The time scale of 23 days is interesting as conception might have taken place on a second cycle if oestrus had not been suppressed in the usual way. My question then was why the hormones associated with parturition had not caused her to abort the twins. Prof Mills speculates that there might be differences in the horns of the uterus to account for this.

It seems the only way to solve the mystery is to commission mitochondrial DNA analysis in the USA which would be prohibitively expensive.

Matilda with her three lambs

Omo is the matriarch of the 'cleaning products 'dynasty which has tested our ability to find names for the line. Omo features in part one- sheep bites dog story. Her first born Breeze gave birth to twins and we think the first born ,Ariel 'was licked off by Ruby while she was having Ajax and subsequently rejected. However, the next time Breeze had twins she rejected the second born twin ,Surf. It seems that neither birth order or gender informed her choices. Perhaps she decided one at a time was quite enough.

Surf in the kitchen

The founding father of our expanded flock was Faygate Prince. We bought him as a yearling and it took him a while to assert himself with the older, larger wethers such as Shaun. He gave us numerous, well bred healthy offspring and went out regularly for stud duties as described in part one. He was one of a number of sheep that roo and so he went a lifetime without being sheared. The downside has been that he and the 20% of his offspring that roo look like moth eaten rugs for weeks in the spring. Sadly, he developed a foot infection which was treated by the vet but did not improve. The solution was amputation which was carried out between Christmas and New Year. Changing his dressings daily was a challenge as he was a big strong ram, albeit well behaved. Cats and dogs seem to adapt to walking on three legs but the centre of gravity of a ram is further forward so the loss of a front foot was hard to accommodate.

However, he learned to hobble on his stump and was in good condition three years after his operation. Following a fight , he became more frail and and we made the decision that he would have to be put down. The vet was kneeling down by him with a loaded syringe when she announced that his heart had stopped.

I never set out to keep sheep but as I came to know them as individuals I became interested in their behaviour and they took over from dogs, horses and cats as the main focus of my observations. As I got to know them as individuals my respect for them grew. I started to write daily field notes about what I had observed and try to understand what guided their activities.

I was surprised how much research had been done around sheep behaviour and realised that understanding them better might lead to more contented sheep, easier to handle and to thrive from a commercial perspective. The downside is that the more one knows and values an individual the more difficult it is to part with them. However, by respecting their social bonds we can make it less stressful for the sheep when they have to move on , if not for their keeper.

I have had many conversations with people who have kept small flocks and knew their sheep as individuals and the stories are fascinating. The ewe who had her lamb with her head on her carers knee or the lamb who lived in the house and followed like a dog. Never underestimate a sheep, just get to know them better.

Reflections and Conclusions

It is curious that of all domestic animals sheep are often singled out as being stupid. They are typically kept in large flocks that are seen as an amorphous mass so that individual variations in behaviour are seldom observed.

To follow like sheep is a pejorative description when applied to human behaviour. In the artificial confines of a field, sheep will often find an escape route through a hedge or fence that their warders have not noticed. They will follow an experienced socially well connected leader in whom they have confidence out of the field in search of more promising forage. In our crowded island escaping sheep are viewed as both a nuisance and a hazard for traffic. In goats such behaviour is seen as enterprising and we admire the elephant herd that follows their experienced matriarch in search of new browse or a water hole. With their well developed awareness of their physical environment sheep demonstrate good navigation skills. As the advisor of Bo-Peep asserted' leave them alone and they'll come home wagging their tails behind them'.

As prey animals, sheep have a dominant flight response to any perceived threat. At round up time or in the presence of strangers they will choose to run and this may be perceived, at best, as inconvenient for their handlers. A straw pole of why people think that sheep are stupid yielded the comment that they might ' follow each other off a cliff or something' This is a theme depicted in the book 'Far from the Madding Crowd' and shown in the various film versions of the book. A similar flight response to a real or perceived threat in a crowd of humans can lead to tragedy as people are crushed in the melee.

In contrast to the popular myths, the research tells us that sheep have the same neurology and brain anatomy as humans and other mammals. They share the same sensory awareness except that the salience of the information from the senses is analysed in a more balanced way and is not dominated by visual input as it is in humans.

Sheep are emotionally and socially intelligent animals that establish long term relationships within their flock. The ewe lamb bond is particularly strong and enduring.

They are skilled communicators using, predominantly, body language but also responding to auditory signals and smell. Face recognition for other sheep and humans is well developed and endures over time. The emotional significance of different facial expressions is recognised and influences their behaviour towards humans and other sheep. Eye contact has a particularly significant role in communication.

Carers and other sheep are remembered even if there has been no contact for up to two years and, possibly, longer. Memory not only for faces but also places and routines is strong. Fortunately, they are also quick to adapt to new routines when they are introduced.

In terms of animal intelligence, sheep function effectively within their natural environment but their ability to take on different cognitive challenges is impressive. They understand and respond to symbolic representation in the form of photographs of sheep and humans and to objects of reference. An object of reference is an object that signifies a future action or event such as excitement at the sight of a bucket. For a dog or Oberon the sight of the lead rope signals the promise of a walk.

Beyond the real life context, sheep are able to solve novel problems set by humans such as mazes or respond to photographs , even images on a computer screen, in order to obtain a reward. The ultimate test of the attention shift paradigm which involves executive function is solved as efficiently by sheep as by humans and monkeys.

Attitudes towards all animals have become more respectful over time as our understanding of their abilities and needs has grown. It is no longer possible to defend the idea that humans are different from animals in some unique way. Animal welfare legislation in the UK has been gradually strengthened since the 1822 Act to Prevent the Improper Treatment of Cattle and the more generic Animal Protection Act of 1911. The Animal Welfare (Sentencing) Bill is the most recent welcome development in this area. Compassion in World Farming, founded in the UK 1967, has a focus on the welfare of farm animals and campaigns against the trend towards factory farming. Fortunately sheep, unlike cows, pigs and hens, have so far largely escaped the abuse of intensive rearing in confined spaces. They are social, intelligent animals that deserve our respect as much as the pets that share our homes. In future you may wince when you hear people call sheep stupid and choose to challenge those assertions.

Never underestimate a sheep.

REFERENCES

Beausoleil, N.J., Blanche, D., Stafford, K. J., Mellor, D.J., Noble, A. D., (20012). Selection for temperament in sheep. Applied Animal Behaviour Science,139(1-2),74-85.

Beausoleil, N.J.,Stafford, K.J., Mellor, D.J.,(2006). Does direct human eye contact function as a warning cue for domestic sheep? Journal of Comparative Psychology 120(3)

Beckoff, M.(2005). The question of animal emotions: An ethnological perspective. In F.D. McMillan (Ed). Mental health and well-being in animals (p.15-28)Blackwell.

Boissy, A., Dumont,B.,(2002). Interactions between social and feeding motivations on the grazing behaviour of herbivores: Sheep more easily split into subgroups with familiar peers. Applied Animal Behaviour Science, 79(3),(233-245)

Bouissou, M. F., Porter, R.H., Boyle, L., Ferreira, G. (1996). Influence of a con specific image of own self. different breed on fear reaction in ewes. Behavioural Processes, 38(1),37-44

Broad, K.D., Mimmack, M. L., Kendrick,K.M. (2000). Is right hemisphere specialisation for face discrimination specific to humans? European Journal of Neural Science,12(2),7310-741

da Costa, A.P. ,Leigh, A.E., Man, M.S., Kendrick,K.M.(2004). Face pictures reduce behavioural, autonomic, endocrine and neural indices of stress and fear in sheep. Proceedings of the Royal Society B: Biological Sciences, 271(1552), 2077-2084.

Davis, H., Norris, C., Taylor,A., (1998). Whether ewe know me or not: The discrimination of individual humans by sheep. Behavioural Processes,43(1),27-32.

De Grazia, D.(2009). Self awareness in animals. George Washington University

De Waal, F.B.M.,(2003) On the possibility of animal empathy. In Manstead, Frieda, Fisch (Ed's). Feelings and emotions: The Amsterdam symposium (377-399). Cambridge University Press

Dwyer, C.,Lawrence, A.B.,(2000) Maternal behaviour in domestic sheep.: constancy and change with maternal experience. Behaviour,137(10), 1391-1413.

Dwyer, C.(2004) How has the risk of predation shaped the behavioural response of sheep to fear and distress. Animal Welfare, 15

Erhard,H.W.(2003). Assessing the relative aversiveness of two stimuli. Single sheep in arena test. Animal Welfare 12

Elliker,K.R.,(2005). Social cognition and its implications for the welfare of sheep. Ph.D thesis. University of Cambridge.

Fails,A.D., McGee,C.(2018) Anatomy and Physiology of Farm Animals.

Ginane, E.C., Dumont,B. (2011). Do sheep categorise plant species according to botanical family? Animal Cognition,14(3),369-376.

Goodall, J.1967. My friends the wild chimpanzees. Washington D.C.:National Geographic Society.

Goodall, J. (1986) The chimpanzees of Gombe: patterns of behaviour. Cambridge M A. Belknap

Griffin,A.S., Evans, C.S.,Blumstein,D.J.(2001) Learning specificity in acquired predator recognition. Animal Behaviour 62

Hinch, G.N. (1989) The suckling behaviour of triplet, twin and single lambs at pasture. Applied Animal Behavioural Science, 22, 39-48

Hinch, G.N., Lecrivain, E., Lynch, J.J., Edwin, R.L.(1987). Changes in maternal young associations with increasing age of lambs. Applied Behavioural Science ,17 305-318.

Kendrick, K.M., Atkinson,K., Hinton,M.R., Broad,K.D., Fabre-Nys,C., Keverne, E.B.,(1995). Facia and vocal discrimination in sheep. Animal Behaviour,49,1665-1676.

Kendrick, K.M., da Costa, A.P., Leigh, A.E., Pearce, J.W.(2001). Sheep don't forget a face. Nature,414(6860),165-166

Kendrick, K.M., da Costa, A.P., Broad, K.D., Ohkura, S., Guevara, R., Levy,F., Kaverne, E.B.,(1997). Neural control of maternal behaviour and olfactory recognition of offspring. Brain Research Bulletin, 44, 383-395.

Knolle, F.,Goncalves,R.P.,Morton,A.J.,(2017). Sheep recognise familiar and unfamiliar human faces from two dimensional images. Royal Society Open Science, 4,171228.

Marino,L., Merskin, D.,(2019). A review of cognition, emotion and social complexity in sheep. Animal Sentience.

Morton,J., Avazo L. (2011). Executive decision making in the domestic sheep. PL05 One,6(1)e15752

Novak,R., Poindron, P., Putu, I.G.,(1989). Development of mother discrimination by single and multiple newborn lambs. Developmental Psychobiology,22(8),833-845.

Parrott, R.F., Misson, B.M.,De la Riva, C.F. (1994) Differential stressor effects on the concentrations of cortisol, prolactin and catecholamines in the blood of sheep. Res.Vet. Sci. 56 234-239.

Pierce,J.W., Leigh, A., daCosta, A.P., Kendrick, K.M.(2001). Human face recognition in sheep: lack of configurational coding and right hemisphere advantage. Behavioural Processes,55(1),13-26.

The Psychologist 2015 vol 28 (11).Genes for face recognition.

Ramseyer, A., Boissy, A., Thierry, B., Dumont,B. (2009). Individual and social determinants of spontaneous group movements in cattle and sheep. Animal,3(9),1319-1326

Reefmann, N., Kaszas, F.B.,Wechler, B., Gygax, L.,(2009) Ear and tail postures as indicators of emotional valence in sheep. Applied Animal Behavioural Science,118(3/4) 199-207

Ripley, K.,(2013) Inclusion for Children with Dyspraxia/ DCD. Fulton

Ripley, K., Barrett, J., (2008). Supporting Speech Language and Communication Needs. Sage

Ripley, K.,(2014). Exploring Friendships , Puberty and Relationships. Jessica Kingsley.

Ripley, K (2015) Autism from Diagnostic Pathway to Intervention. Jessica Kingsley

Ripley, K., Murphy, R., (2020) Getting the Best out of College for Students on the Autism Spectrum. Jessica Kingsley

Ritcher, H.(2004) Friendly faces calm stressed sheep. Nature on Line.

Rowell, T.E.,(1991) Till death do us part: long lasting bonds between ewes and their daughters. Animal Behaviour,42, 681-682.

Safini ,C.(,2015) Beyond Words.What animals think and feel. Pub Henry Holt, New York.

Schauder, K.B., Mash,L.E., Bryant, L.K., Cassio, C.(2015) Interoceptive ability and body awareness in Autistic Spectrum Disorder. Journal of Experimental Child Psychology.131. 193-200

Sebe, F., Aubin,T., Poindon, P.(2008) Mother and young communication and acoustic recognition promote preferential nursing in sheep. Journal of Experimental Biology 211.

Shackleton,D.M., Shank.C.C.(1984) A review of the social behaviour of feral and wild sheep and goats. Journal of Animal Science,58(2),500-509.

Sibbald, A.M., Erhard, H.W., McLeod, J.E., Hooper,R.J.(2009). Individual personality and the spatial distribution of groups of grazing animals: an example with sheep. Behavioural Proceedings,82,391-326.

Vandenheede, M., Bouissou, M.F.(1994). Fear reactions of ewes to photographic images. Behavioural Processes,32(1),17-28

Villalba,J.J., Provenza, F.D., Shaw,R. (2006) Sheep self-medicate when challenged with illness inducing foods. Animal Behaviour,71(5),1131-1139.

Printed in Great Britain
by Amazon

85441206R00058